CW01262921

Introduction to the book

This book is intended to introduce hair stylists not only to the practical aspect of braiding, but also the professional and theoretical background of braiding. After extensive research and practice at the Hair? Braid it! salon we discovered that there is more to braiding than just installing a plait. This book was developed to share knowledge, with hopes of standardizing the braiding industry and creating a professional atmosphere.

Writers

This book was written by Afiya Hopson, a hair stylist with years of experience in braiding and teaching in her salon and workshops.

Editors

This book was creatively edited by Makini Hughes and grammatically edited by Liseli James.

Acknowledgements

Without the help of family, friends, and teammates, this book would not be possible. Over the years I created workshops that helped to educate women about the art of braiding. I creatively constructed notes and quizzes to allow students to become professional in a short period of time. Students were often impressed by the notes, and encouraged me to turn it into a book. Thanks to my clients for your support over the years. Your love and pictures on social media have helped this business to flourish into the creation of this book. Thank you to my teammates, for supporting my dream and giving me tips and ideas along the way. To my family, I thank you for your willingness to promote me every step of the way; I owe it all to you. A special thank you to my daughter, your presence, love and joy you bring to my life, gave me the strength to complete this project.

Copyright

The book was written by Afiya Hopson of Hair? Braid it! Salon.

Company information

Name: Hair? Braid It!

Number: 868-221-2424 / 868-477-0659

Email: hairbraidit@gmail.com

Website: hairbraidit.com

Location: Port-of-Spain, Trinidad

Table of Contents

Part 1- Introduction

1. Background on Braids… Pg 7
2. Hair Care for Braids…….Pg 11

Part 2- Braiding Essentials

3. Tools…………………….Pg 13
4. Products……………….....Pg 16
5. Braid lengths………..…..Pg 18
6. Braid Types……………..Pg 20
7. Colours……………...…..Pg 23

Part 3- Braid Installation

8. Plaits- three strand plait…Pg 25

9. Twists-two strand method..Pg 38
10. Cornrows………………..Pg 44
11. Braiding Don't's………..Pg 51
12. Finishing the style……..Pg 52

Part 4- Professionalism

13. Salon set up……………Pg 54
14. Time management……..Pg 54
15. The client……………….Pg 56
16. Running a business…….Pg 57

Review Questions..................Pg 59

Part One: Introduction

1. About Braids

Braiding is the interweaving of strands of hair, often using hair extensions and although it has recently gained popularity, the style itself has been around for centuries among different countries and cultures. No surprise that the hairstyle, which is sported mostly among Afro-Caribbean's and African Americans, is said to have originated centuries ago on the African continent with many photos emerging of both Nubian men and women wearing the style.

The origins of braids go all the way back to 3500BCE. The styles were commonly seen on both men and women and it was often used as a symbol of glamour, social and marital status, ethnicity and religious affliction. The styles that existed in old centuries played a major role in history. The style often indicated a person's kingship, age, ethnicity and religion.

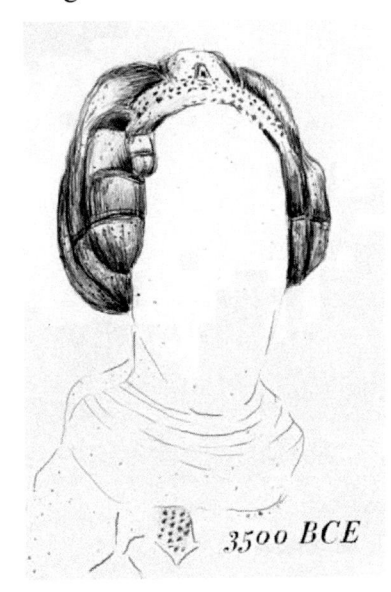

Picture 1-1

In more recent times, braiding is used by many of its wearers as a protective style for their hair. They often use braids to prevent damage, especially in extreme climates.

However, this style, once marketed and executed correctly can be worn throughout the year. In fact, the demand for braids continues to grow due to the recent Natural Hair Movement. Black women are trying to maintain a lot more chemical-free hairstyles and braiding is often selected as a choice to encourage these efforts. Braids are a very good choice for women, but it must be done correctly and stylists must become well educated about the style and the client before proceeding with the service.

Braid extensions became internet famous with the surge of YouTube video releases in 2005. Many of the styles throughout the book stem from past cultures and countries which are now modernized and very popular.

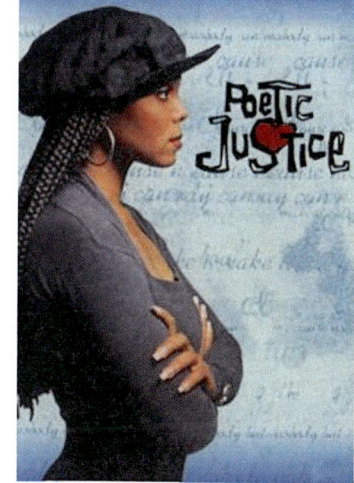

Picture 1-2   Picture 1-3

In the 90's braids were very popular, and celebrities like Beyoncé and Janet Jackson created trends that still are popular today, such as "The Poetic Justice Braids" as shown in Picture 1-3. There was a drop in the demand for braids in the new millennium, but braids in the Caribbean were always in high demand during seasons like carnival (see picture 1-5) and July-August vacation see picture (1-4), to give trendy manageable styles during these warmer and busier seasons. It was also demanded by expecting mothers or mothers who were breast feeding, as during this time they are advised by their doctors not to use chemicals, and braid styles were a good choice.

Picture 1-4:   Picture1-5

Fast forward ten years into the new millennium, braids regained its popularity, not only because of the previously mentioned Natural Hair Movement, but also because of new technologies. The style itself became more modernized, and took shorter times, with revolutionary designs. Braids are now available in many lengths, curls, textures and colours, and even ombre colours, as shown in Picture 1-6a and b. The style has also expanded beyond its core group of wearers, with women of other ethnicities preferring a braid style with extensions because it gives them versatility, volume and length at cheaper costs for a much longer time. Thus, a style that was traditionally demanded by black women is now demanded by all women, as any hair texture can wear braid extensions once a suitable style is chosen. In picture 1-7 we show you a German model wearing Senegalese twists.

Picture 1-6a   b   Picture 1-7

It is very important that stylists understand hair types, density and texture to effectively install different braiding styles. If the braiding style chosen is not a suitable choice for the person's hair then the style can become destructive. Why? The tension and weight of the synthetic hair can damage the hairline or multiple parts of the hair causing alopecia. For example, new mothers who often demand braids (for its convenience) often experience post-partum alopecia (hair loss) during breast-feeding, as seen in Picture 1-8. So it is important that stylists advise whether or not a braiding style is the healthiest option for the client, and if so, which style in particular is most appropriate for their hair. Another example is moisture, hair that is not sufficiently moisturized before installation of braids can easily break after the braids are installed. It is therefore important that stylists understand the right amount of moisture the client's hair needs, so that hair is neither too dry, nor too moist to install the style. In general, it is the responsibility of the stylist to ensure that the braiding style is not only what the client wants, but also what is best for the health of the client's hair. Unfortunately, in some cases that means that after a thorough hair and scalp analysis is conducted, you may decide that the braiding style may not be the best option for your client at that time.

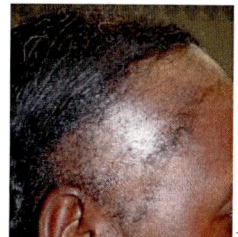

Picture 1-8

2. Hair care for Braids

Six simple steps to a successful braiding experience

I. Pre-braid installation: Always wash deep condition, de-tangle, dry and moisturize your hair no more than 3 days before your appointment. Use appropriate shampoos to clarify and treat the hair before the service, especially if there is any chemical damage to the hair.

Recommendations: Try to use sulfate-free shampoos to retain moisture in the hair.

II. Wearing the style: Use rubber bands as shown in Picture 2-1 or very stretchy hair ties ("woogie") to put your braid in an up-do, it reduces the amount of strain on your hairline. Recommendations: Some braids come with strong rubber bands that will help hold the hair together without bursting. Store these for clients.

2-1; rubber bands

III. Sleeping: When going to bed try to place all hair in a one and wrap your hair in a bun see picture 2-2 and then tie with a hair tie as shown in picture 2-3 so that all the hair is covered. Recommendations: Use a silk hair tie. However, if hair extensions are very long and the bun becomes very heavy, leave hair down and place in a satin cap as shown in picture 2-4.

Picture 2-2    Picture 2-3; silk hair tie    Picture 2-4; Satin sleep cap

IV. Maintenance: Moisten your scalp and use hair boosters on the hairline. Recommendations: Natural oils and hair serums are good options choose one that does not irritate your scalp.

V. Washing: Try to place hair up in a one and wrap in a bun as shown in picture 2-2, focus on the roots of your hair and minimize wetting ends to ensure braids stay neat. Recommendations: The styles you can easily wash while your braids remain fairly neat are; Box braids, patra braids, faux locs, marley twists, cuban twists, afro kinky and small senegalese twists.

VI. Removal: for short hair you can cut the braids to a length a little longer than your hair and unloose, unless you would like to reuse the hair for another installation (then you unplait from the end). Only certain braids can be re-used. If your hair is long unloose braids from the end. After removing the braids, start to detangle hair; a spray bottle (Picture 2-3) with water should be nearby to assist with detangling. The spray bottle will help control the amount of water applied. One should never shampoo their hair before de-tangling unless it is their usual routine. This can cause hair damage and hair loss. The best option is to use your fingers to de-tangle each plait and reduce hair loss. Recommendations: Braids should be left in no longer than 4-8 weeks unless advised differently by your hairstylist.

Picture 2-5; Spray bottle

Part two: Braiding Essentials

3. Tools

To perform the braid service there are some tools that most braid stylists will use in their studio or salon. The following are tools that you may need to effectively complete a braid style from start to finish.

- ✓ Mug (with handle): to safely hold water when dipping the ends of the braid.
- ✓ Towels: used to drape clients and to hold braids when wet.
- ✓ Shampoo cape: to drape client.
- ✓ Apron: for the stylist to wear.
- ✓ Hairdressing scissors: For clipping and cutting braids.
- ✓ Rattail comb: For parting.
- ✓ Afro comb: To detangle hair or help strip braids.
- ✓ Shampoo Comb: to detangle hair or to help strip braids.
- ✓ Pin curl clips; for sectioning hair for control.
- ✓ Duck bill clips: for sectioning hair for control.

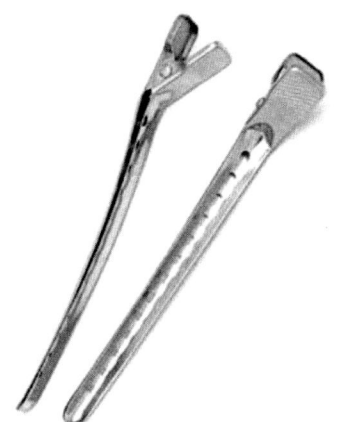

Picture 3-1; Duck bill clips

- ✓ Bobby pins; for styling.
- ✓ Hair pins: for styling.
- ✓ Jerry curlers : number of different sizes to curl ends of some braids.

Most tools will be used on a daily basis, and some are just for certain looks but should always be kept handy just in case such as:

- ✓ Electric kettle: Braids are manipulated by boiling water this is used by most styles to crimp, curl or straighten ends. It makes the braid neater and gives the braid movement. An electric kettle is necessary to provide hot water quickly to do the finishing touches.
- ✓ Sanitizing Jar: sanitize all tools that can be re-used.

Picture 3-2; Sanitizing Jar

- ✓ Flexi Rods Number of different sizes to curl ends of some braids.

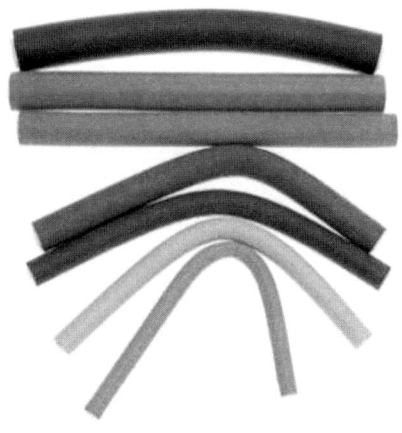

Picture 3-3; Flexi rods

- ✓ Blow dryer: to dry clients natural hair and braid extensions.

- ✓ Crochet/ interlocking needle: to install crochet braids.

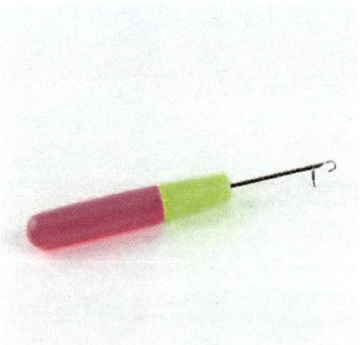

Picture 3-4; Crochet needle

- ✓ Weave needle : to secure hair before a crochet style.

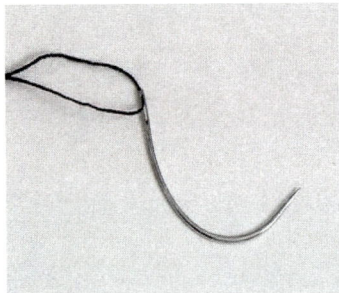

Picture 3-5; Weave needle and thread

- ✓ Weave thread: to secure hair before a crochet style.

4. Hair Products

Always try to read the labels on any hair products you use. It is recommended to use products that are listed as alcohol-free, as products with alcohol tend to irritate the scalp and dry out hair. Remember any product you use will be applied throughout the client's hair and will stay in for roughly four weeks, so select your products wisely! Different brands are available across the world, so pick the one which is best for you.

- ✓ Braid sheen spray- provides the finishing touches.
- ✓ Hair Spritz- keeps hair in place, good for cornrow styles.
- ✓ Braid spray- moistens scalp.
- ✓ Hair mousse (non alcoholic)- defines curls to get rid of any extra pieces of hair that the naked eye cannot see. There are different types, curl activators and shine and hold. Try to have the two handy.
- ✓ Hair Jam (non alcoholic)- holds hair in place for most individual plait hairstyles it makes the style more manageable and gives an extra shine. Some clients may prefer another option depending on their hair type. Picture 4-1;Shine jam non alcoholic
- ✓ Moisturizer- softens the hair and is usually applied before drying.
- ✓ Detangler- detangles hair and assists with parting for the style during the braid service.
- ✓ Edge Control- assists with the hairline to get the short pieces neatly placed in the braid.
- ✓ Taming gel- used for cornrows mainly goddess and glamour to hold hair in place.
- ✓ Hair oil- adds moisture to hair after applying heat.

- ✓ Shampoo- assists with cleansing the hair. Sulfate free shampoos and special shampoos to deal with multiple hair conditions should be kept handy to ensure maximum results.
- ✓ Conditioner- assists with moisturizing hair or straightening the hair strand. Also have a deep conditioner available to go with the multiple shampoos you may have available

This is list is just a guide you may or may not need everything listed in your studio.

5. Braid Lengths

There are several types of braids which are all packaged differently. Some braids come in specified length while others may need to be cut to achieve the desired length. Inches are also differently represented when textures are compared. Below, I have constructed tables, which will help you to achieve the desired length based on the type of hair you as using.

Table 5-1; Super X kankelon

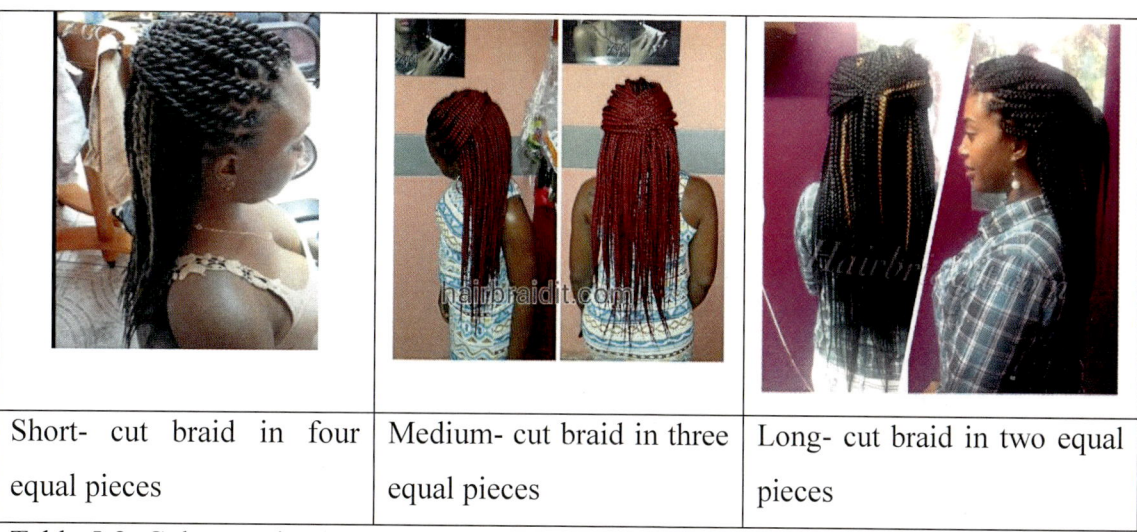

Short- cut braid in four equal pieces	Medium- cut braid in three equal pieces	Long- cut braid in two equal pieces

Table 5-2; Cuban Twists/ Marley twists

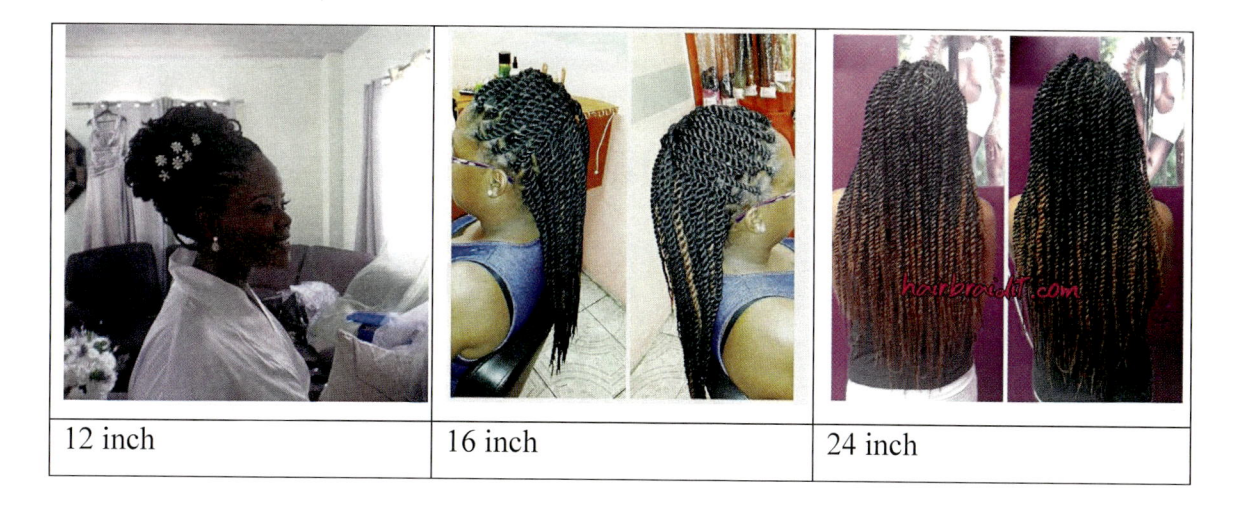

12 inch	16 inch	24 inch

Table 5-3; Afro kinky

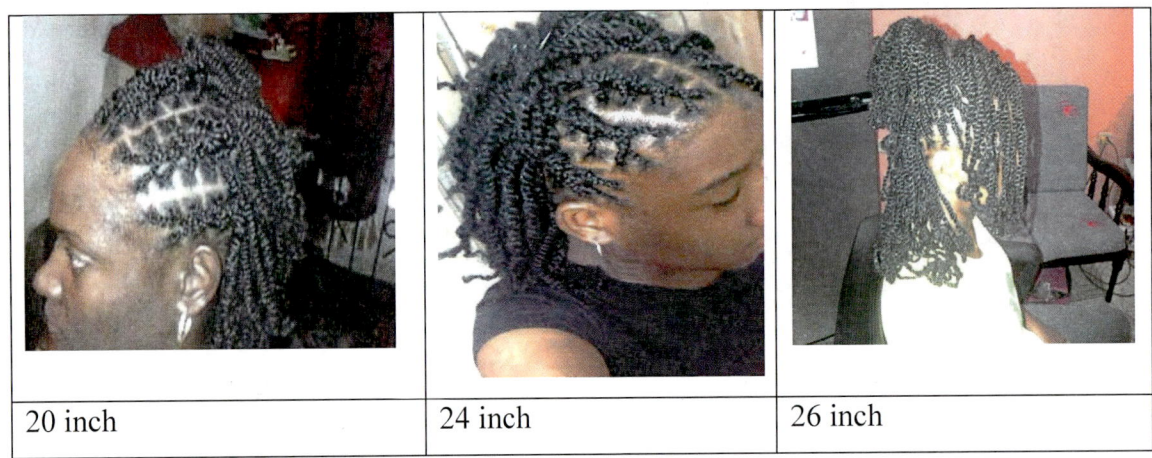

20 inch	24 inch	26 inch

Table 5-4; Faux / Goddess locs

Shoulder Length	Mid back	Waist length	Hip Length

Table 5-6; Curly braids

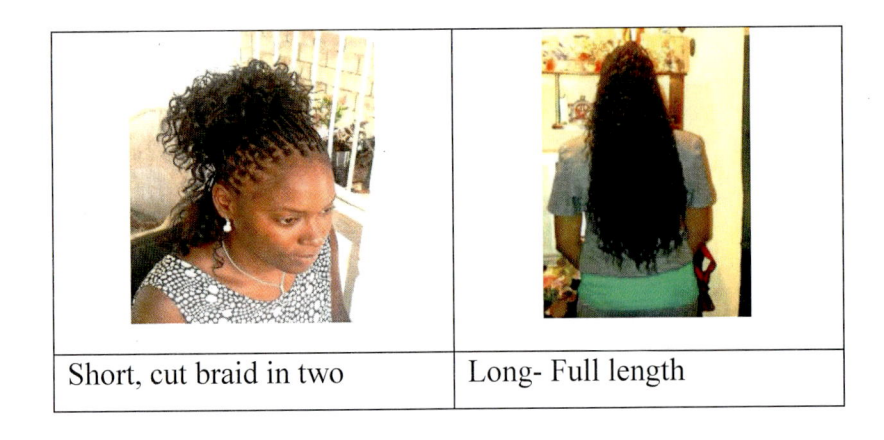

Short, cut braid in two	Long- Full length

6. Braid Types

There are many different brands, types and lengths available in braid extensions. It is important that you use the correct extension to provide maximum results at the end of the service. This section will elaborate on the type of extensions that are available.

- ➤ Jumbo braids are usually the least expensive type of braid on the market. Here are its uses as it pertains to each braiding technique:

  Plaits: It can be used for the base of styles such as faux locs, crochet braids and for pin ups to give volume. It can also be used for box braids but may not give optimal results.

  Twists: It cannot be used. Any braid that is not kankelon fiber will unloose.

  Cornrow: It can be used but may not give optimal results.

- ➤ Jumbo Kankelon braids are the lighter of the two types of kankelon. It is usually used to create softer looks and is used for all techniques with some modifications involved. It is available in various brands and it is important for you to select the best type for the task at hand. This braid is a very good option for persons who request lighter styles, have thinning hair or if they have fine hair strands.

Picture 6-1; Jumbo Kankelon on fine hair

- Super x Kankelon braids are the heavier of the two types of kankelon. It comes in longer lengths and gives much neater and voluminous hairstyles. However, it is heavier than the others and not all hair textures should use it as it may cause damage. It is used for all braiding techniques with the appropriate modifications.

Picture 6-2; Super x kankelon using plait technique.

- Marley Braids/ Jamaican braid or Afro twists is similar to natural hair and usually comes in longer lengths. It is separated by strands. This is used for twisting, some types of crochet braids and the final hair used to create Goddess/ faux locs as shown in table 5-4. It is an excellent choice for natural hair types to blend into the hair more naturally.
- Cuban twists have similar features to marley twists however it comes in lengths 12inch, 16 inch and 24inch. It is a bit thicker than marley and less strands are needed to give a thick look. It is perfect for thick natural hair that can withstand its weight and is only used for twisting, some types of crochet braids and the final hair used to create Goddess/ faux locs.

Picture 6-3; Cuban twists on natural hair.

- Curly braids are usually used for crochet braids, for the base of goddess locs and for the clients who want small plaits and the ends left out. It helps clients with natural hair get a look similar to some weaves without having to leave there hairline out. Commonly found in the freetress brand.

Picture 6-4; Gogo curl

- Crochet braids: Though all braid types can be more or less crocheted in to the clients hair there are some that are specifically created for crocheting and there is a loop at the end so that the hair is easily installed. A common crochet braid is mambo jumbo twists. These braids are easy to install and are relatively quick. This is also known as the braided weave.
- Afro Kinky/ Kinky Bulk is commonly used on natural hair and stylists can plait at the top and twist at the ends or twists from the roots as shown in Picture 5-3. It is also used for crochet braids and faux locs.

7. Colour

Example of a good colour chart, do your research on other braid colour charts that exist.

Picture 7-1; Colour chart

The way colour is described in braids is a bit different to what is in the hair colouring chapter of your average cosmetology book. For one, the numbering in a braid chart is different and so too are the shades which are modified when compared to chemical colouring. Braids colours can range from 1-613 and should be learnt to show that the stylist is well educated about what exists on the market. In each brand of braids the shades may vary.

Picture 7-3; Colour 613; platinum blonde

Picture 7-2; I305 & 35

Part 3: Braid installation

This section will introduce you to the three strand method of braiding. This type of braiding usually stays neater for a longer period of time when compared to other methods.

8. Plaits

<u>Portioning</u>

This section will briefly discuss how many packs of braids stylists will need for particular styles. We should refer a lot to the length charts that we previously discussed in Part 2, 5.

- Box braids: Short-2/3packs; Medium-3/4packs; Long-3.5-5 packs. This refers to when Super x kankelon is used.
- Nubian/ Faux locs: At least one pack of super x to every three packs of marley hair, this will vary depending on the desired length.

Picture 8-1;Mid-back faux locs

- Afro-Kinky; 3-4 packs in any length, they are offered in 12", 20" 24" & 26"

- Patra braids: Medium- 4-5packs Long 5-6packs Super x kankelon. This style is not offered in short due to the thickness that is required. It is recommended that it is only done in longer lengths.

Picture 8-2;Long all black patra

- Goddess Locs: a pack of super x kankelon, a pack of free tress curls and 3 packs marley hair, depending on the thickness & length desired this will always vary.
- Curly braids: 2-3 packs for short braids are cut in half to get this length, 3-5packs for long.

Remember depending on the thickness of a client's hair you will have to adjust the portions you add in each particular plait to obtain suitable results.

Preparation

i. How to cut the super x braid to achieve lengths:

Short; bra strap length- cut braid in four equal pieces

Medium; mid-back- cut braid in three equal pieces

Long; waist length- Cut braid in 2 equal pieces

ii. There are two ways to split braids into three.

1. Take one side and split it in two. This is used for curly braids and Afro kinky, to minimize the chance of braids getting knots.

    Picture 8-3; Split one side in two pieces.

2. Separate the braid into two pieces, ensuring one piece is half the size of the other, and then place the smaller of the two pieces over the center of the thicker piece so that it is now doubled see picture 8-4a. Then, hold the two small pieces that you just placed on top together as one so that it will appear as three pieces will refer to picture 8-4b. This technique is used for Patra braids and box braids.

    Always try to be delicate when preparing either braid.

    Picture 8-4; three equal pieces.

Picture 8-3   Picture 8-4a   Picture 8-4b

iii. Teasing Super X braids for patra braids or box braids.

Hold hair in left hand tightly, using all your fingers except your thumb as shown in Picture 8-5. Place thumb on top gently ensuring if a force is applied to the braids it will move. Take your right hand and begin to pull small pieces of the blunt ends, this should give the braids an extra 2 inches in length. Keep pulling little blunt ends until there are little to no blunt edges visible giving a feathered look see picture 8-6. Detangle hair with hands then comb through with a shampoo comb or a tool of your choice.

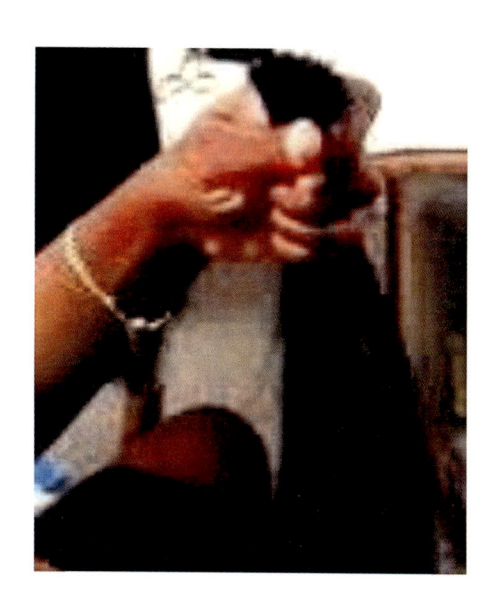

Picture 8-5; How to hold

Picture 8-6 final product

Parting

Section parting- this is for control

Part hair in two: using the top of the ear as your guide at all times.

Section parting must be done first in order to get defined individual parts.

Picture 8-7;Section part

Individual parting for squares.

Straight horizontal lines are required to part rows out. Always part an entire row at a time so that parts are straight and even. When horizontal parts are completed then do vertical lines to get individual parts and use clips to hold them in place.

Picture 8-8; Individual parts

Picture 8-9; box braids

Individual parting for equilateral triangular parts

Start from a corner of a person's hair preferably the right back corner and part diagonally as shown in picture 8-10. This should give one or two plaits. To get multiple plaits from this, diagonal part the opposite direction into the number of plaits you desire. This is usually parted bigger than other braids to sustain the weight applied. Continue this pattern until midway of the back of the person's hair then start all over in the opposite corner parting in the other direction. A corner should be easily identified, when the back is finished start this technique in the front this is shown in Picture 8-11.

Picture 8-10; Diagonal part

Picture 8-11; diagonal part

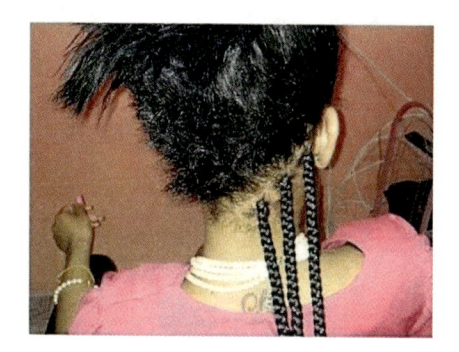

Installing a braid

Braiding is a cyclic motion which tends to use your both hands and all your fingers. The hands are made up of the working fingers which are the index, the thumb and sometimes the middle finger and the rest are considered the storage fingers which are the ring finger and pinky finger.

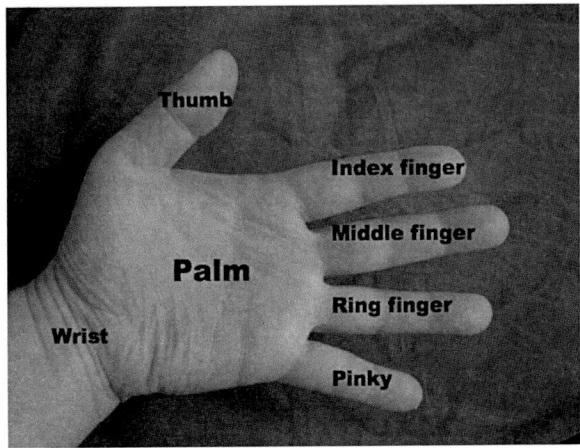

Picture 8-12; Picture of hand.

Before we start to braid we must first understand how to plait on natural hair. How do you plait? Inside or Outside?

A plait is a constant rotation using three equal pieces of hair using your both hands throughout the plait. It is important that you understand that there are inside and outside plaits. Outside plaits is what you will be using to install plait braids. The difference between the two is the direction in which each piece is rotated.

Now try this simple exercise!

1. Part a 1cm row at the back of the client's hair.
2. Create 4 to 5 vertical parts ensuring that they are equal squares. NOT rectangles they must be squares.
3. Split the hair in the square into three different pieces placing one piece in the right hand and the other two pieces in the left or vice versa.
4. Take the piece of hair in the middle and carry it over the piece at the far right. (the right piece will now become the middle piece) At the same time hold the piece that you just moved and put it between your middle and ring finger. See picture 8-13a.
5. Take your index finger and move the new center piece over the piece of hair at the far left and hold this piece between the middle finger and the index finger. At the same time, try to take the right index finger and pull the new center piece over the far right piece of hair. See picture 8-13b
6. Continue this motion till the hair ends.

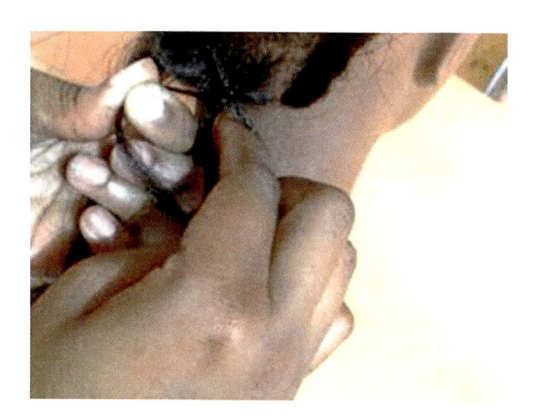

Picture 8-13a 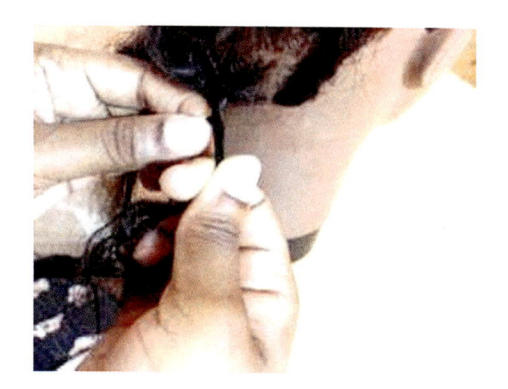   Picture 8-13b

Adding braiding extensions

Step 1: Hold the braid in three, one piece is held in your left hand, another piece (preferably the folded piece) is held in your right hand between your ring finger and middle finger and the last piece is held between your index finger and middle finger. This may vary if you are left handed.

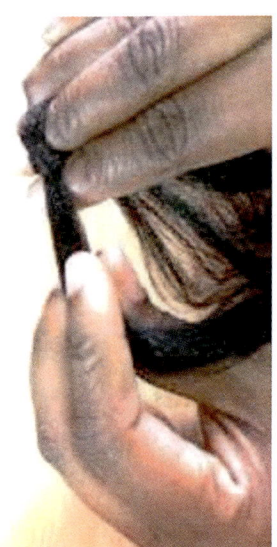

Picture 8-14; Step 1

Step 2: Keep the braid secure in hands and place on the hair that is parted, split hair in three equal pieces and match it up with the braids ensuring that they are held together in the same manner between the fingers.

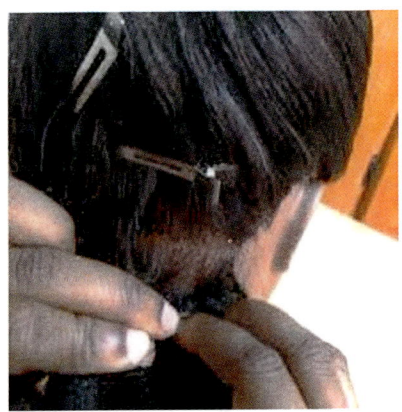

Picture 8-15; Step 2

Step 3: Take the piece of hair in the middle and carry it over the piece at the far right (the right piece will now become the middle piece). At the same time hold the piece that you just moved and put it between your middle and ring finger.

Step 4: Take your index finger and move the new center piece over the piece of hair at the far left and hold this piece between the middle finger and the index finger. At the same time, try to take the right index finger and pull the new center piece over the far right piece of hair.

Remember to keep your knuckles up while doing this and try to press down on the person's hair firmly to keep the braids tight as shown in step 2.

Step 5: Continue this cyclic motion for five times ensuring that you keep your knuckles up. Then, drop knuckles and lower hands and continue the cycle. Always push slightly against the scalp and only lower your hands if the plait allows you to, meaning keep your hands as close to the last cycle as possible to ensure plaits are always tight.

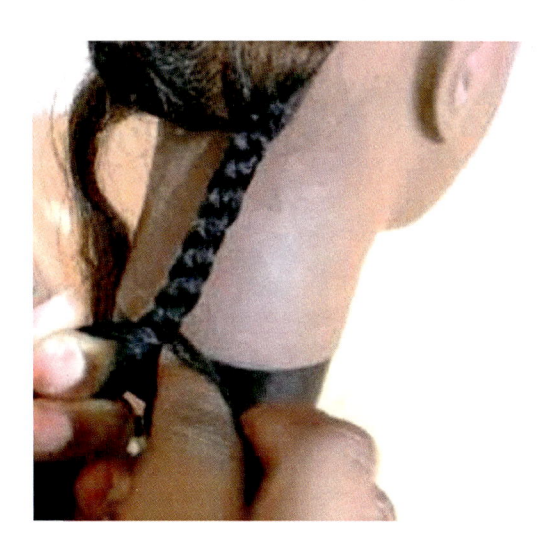

Picture 8-16; Step 5

Afro-kinky braid

When doing afro kinky braid, a plait and twist is required. See modification below:

Picture 8-17; 26 inch Afro kinky

For plait and twist, plait the top for 1-2 inches as described before. Then, transition from plait to twists, when transitioning split one of the sections into two and join each with one of the other pieces of hair and you should remain with two pieces. Begin to twist the braid by simply rolling the braid a bit and then crossing one piece of hair on top of the other.

If the hair is natural, even if you have to plait straight down, try to roll the hair into the braids so it is barely visible, if at all through the braids. Then plait or twist the hair.

Faux locs / Goddess locs

Step 1. Plait hair with a suitable base braid until you pass the client's hair, if the client's hair is very long just plait about 5 inches.

Step 2. When wrapping faux locs take a piece and bend it so that it is lined up with the braids no more than 2 inches hold it tightly in place with the braid at the top and begin to wrap in a circular motion. See picture 8-18a,b &c

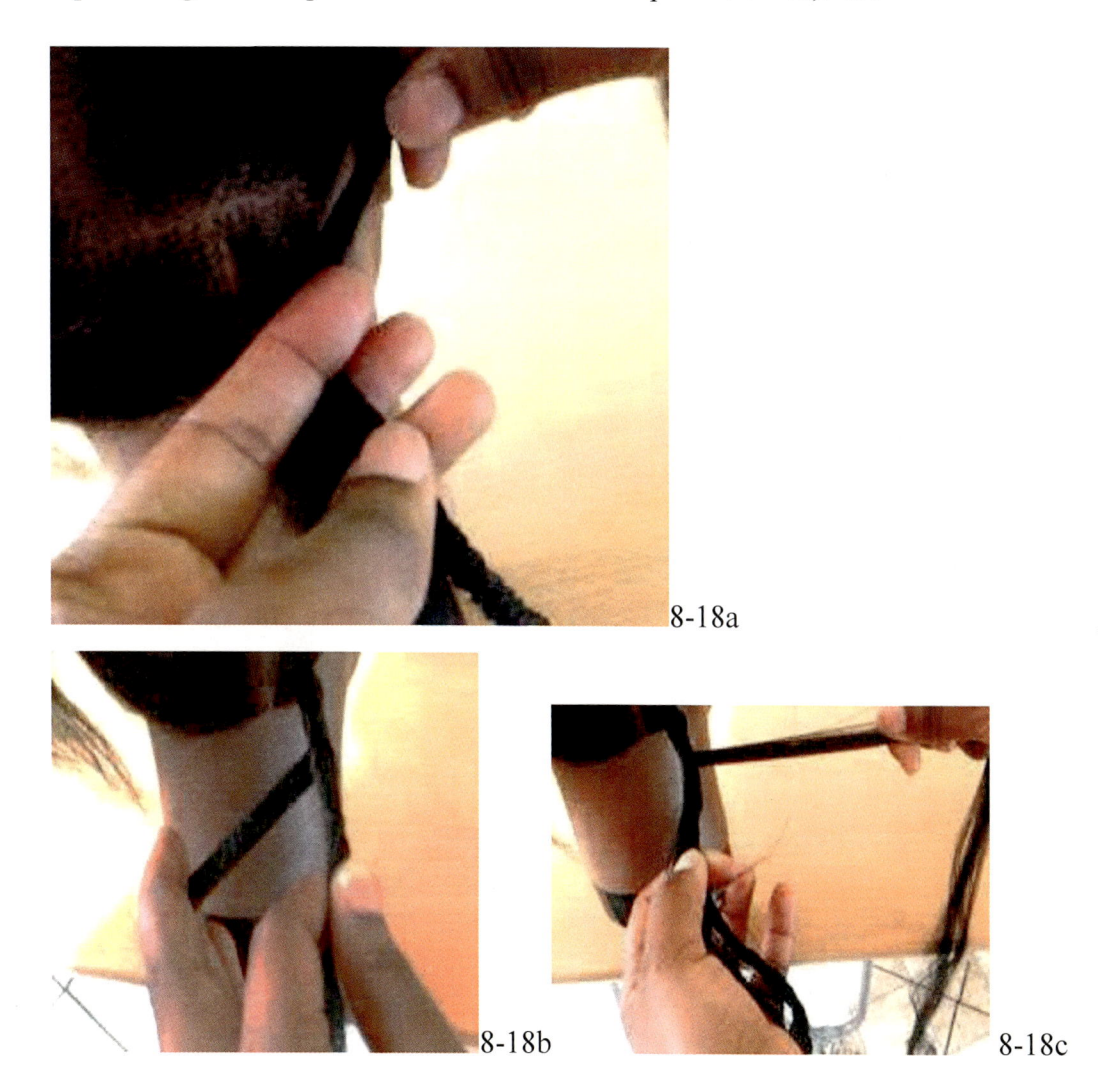

8-18a

8-18b

8-18c

Step 3. Continue wrapping until you are 2cm after the person's hair ends, begin to apply weave glue and continue wrapping till the end. If hair is remaining add glue on the top of the ends and then begin to wrap upwards again. In the case of Goddess locs roughly 1-2 inches of curl is left out at the ends, so that is where the marley should end.

Sometimes, when doing locs, multiple strands have to be added to get the desired length. Simply repeat step 2 when adding a new piece of hair.

You are also not required to tease ends of super x to do faux locs.

Picture 8-19 Faux locs

Picture 8-20 Goddess locs

9. Twists Section

This is a two strand method of braiding. It gives a polished look that is preferred for special events such as dinners. It is very easy to unloose, and it is lighter on the hair strand when compared to the plait method.

Portioning the braids

Senegalese twists

The shorter the person's hair the more braids used, the longer the person's hair, the less braids used. This is something that will vary for each person's head and you need to decide if it is too much or too little to ensure that the braids look thick when they are completed.

Picture 9-1; Long Senegalese twists

The number of packs to prepare for each length for Senegalese twists:

Short- 2.5 packs(Super X braids are cut in four), Medium- 3 packs (braids are cut in three),Long- 4.5 packs (braids are cut in two)

If someone has very light or dougla hair, please use Braid now kankelon (5-7 packs), Que braid (2-3 packs), or Supreme jumbo kankelon braid (5-7 packs)

Havana twists

Three pieces of marley braid are required for each plait. Some clients like their hair thicker so four may be needed. However, when you reach the top- middle of the person's hair four pieces should be used so that the braids look full and fall nicely.

The amount of braids required for Havana twists: 8-12 packs of Marley braids. Depends on the client's hair and the thickness required, and the brand of marley hair you have.

Picture 9-2; Havana Twists

Marley twists

Each plait requires one piece of marley hair depending on how thick the hair itself is. Parts should be roughly 1cm squares but if the client's hair is extremely thin, short or relaxed two pieces in each plait is required especially to the top center of the person's hair.

Picture 9-3; Marley twists using 8 packs of Marley/Jamaican braid

Jumbo Twists

This style is done very thick. The amount of braids in a plait should amount to at least twice the size of your pinky finger. Please portion the braids evenly to get that thick, rope twist look.

The amount of braids required for jumbo Twists: Medium: 4 packs (super x kankelon), long: 5-6 packs.

Because of the thickness of the jumbo twists it is not offered in the short length as the braids will get too thin too quickly and it will not look good.

Picture 9-4; Jumbo Twists

Cuban twists

They are available in three lengths 12inch, 16inch & 24inch

There are three sizes: Small- Box parts with one strand each 5-6 packs, Medium- triangular parts with two strands in each plait 6-7 packs, Large-triangular parts with three strands in each plait 7-8 packs.

Picture 9-5; Cuban Twists

Preparation for twists

    a) Teasing Super X braids for twist styles.

Procedure: Hold hair in left hand tightly but ensure if a force is applied the braids will move. Take right hand and begin to pull on small pieces of the blunt ends, this should give the braids an extra 2 inches of length. Keep doing this until there are little to no blunt edges visible. This is illustrated in Picture 8-6 and 8-7 in the previous section.

    b) Marley and Cuban twists thinning ends

Procedure: Hold hair firmly and use shampoo comb to comb out the ends gently. This will thin out the ends causing the braids to close easier.

Parting

Please refer to parting methods discussed in section 8 Plaits.

Twists installation

Braiding is a cyclic motion which tends to use your both hands and all your fingers. This method consists of the interweaving of two strands by using a rolling method. It is fairly simple to follow, but may be difficult on the hands.

Step 1: Apply jam to the client's hair.

Step 2: Hold the braid in two, one piece is held in you left hand, another piece is held in your right hand, and both pieces are held between your index fingers and thumbs.

Step 3: Keep the braid secure in your hands and place it on the hair that is parted, split hair in two, and match it up with the braid ensuring that they are held together in the same manner between the fingers.

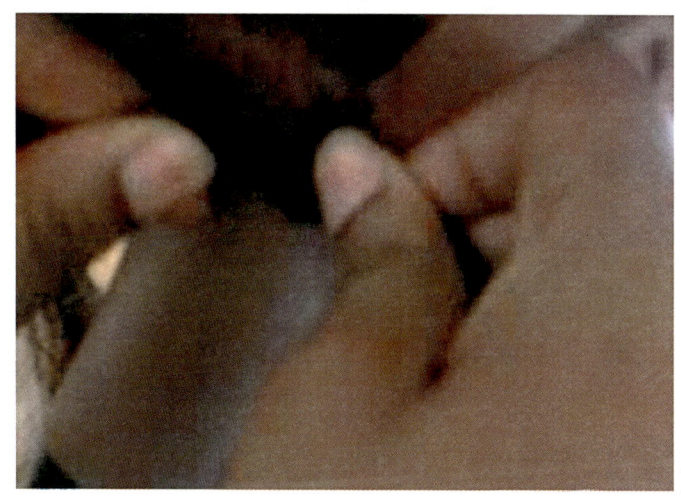

Picture 9-6; Step 1-3

Step 4: Take the piece of hair in the left hand and roll at least three times to the right, if hair is relaxed and four times to the right if hair is natural. Then roll the braid in the left hand three times to the right or four times to the right if hair is natural.

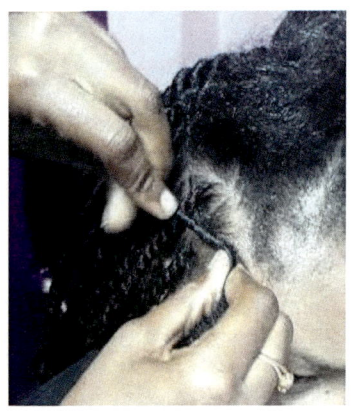

Picture 9-7; Step 4

Step 5: Hold the rolled hair in the right hand tightly while rolling the hair in the left hand. After this is done, begin to cross the braids to the left side which is the opposite direction to what you just rolled. Therefore you will start with the piece in the right hand and carry it over the piece in the left.

Step 6: Keep knuckles up and after each cross roll both pieces to the right tightly before you cross. Cross at least four times with your knuckles up. Then drop your hands continue to ROLL each time before you cross. THIS IS MANDITORY UNTIL THE VERY END OF THE TWIST, OR ELSE IT WILL UNRAVEL.

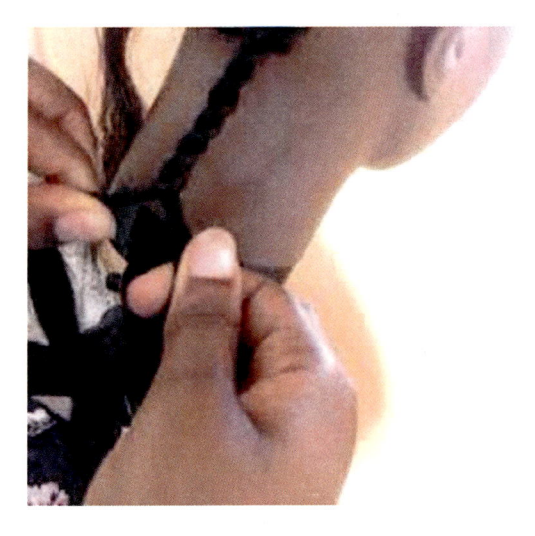

Picture 9-8: step 6

10. Cornrows Section

Picture 10-1; Cornrow updo; Cornrows tend to allow stylist to show their creative side.

A cornrow is a continuation of a plait along a given path. With that being said, you start a cornrow the same way you will start a plait but you just keep your knuckles pressed down to the client's hair throughout the plait. After each rotation you grab up hair directly under to ensure that it does not lift and continue throughout. Always use small portions of hair and plait in the center of the plait. We will look into this with more detail as we go through the steps of the glamour braid next.

Picture 10-2; Glamour cornrows

Glamour Braids Steps

1. Part out roughly 10-15 pieces of braids ensuring that they gradually get bigger after every 2 to 3 pieces ensuring that the very first one starts off with just about a pinch of hair.

Picture 10-3; step 1

2. Begin the cornrow with only the client's hair adding braid at this point can prevent the plait from looking natural and potentially damage the client's hair.

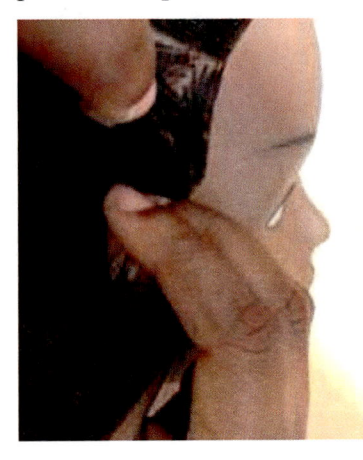

Picture 10-4; step 2

3. After about three full rotations of the cornrow in the given part add the very small piece of hair under the index finger aligning with only two pieces of the client's hair. Please ensure that when you are doing this your index finger is in a position to be lifted without the plait unloosing.

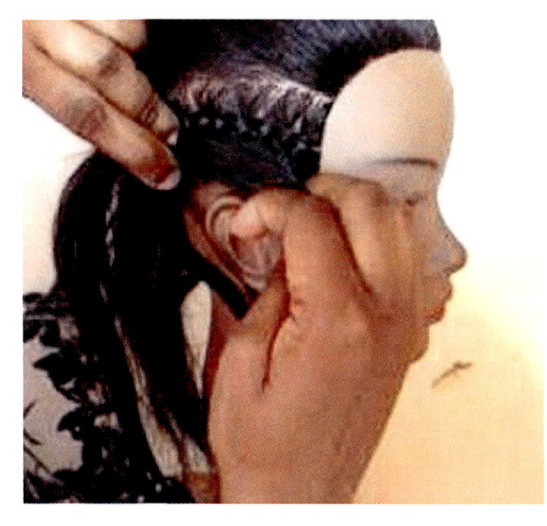

Picture 10-5; step 3

4. Secure this piece of hair with one full rotation and then add another very small piece of hair under the index finger.

5. After every two to four rotations depending on how thick or fine the person's hair is add another piece of hair under the index as stated above.

Picture 10-6; Step 5

6. Continue until you reach the end. When the cornrow is finished, gently comb through the loose hair to determine how much hair needs to be added again to get all three pieces to an even size so that plaits are flush and to also get the desired length. At this point pieces are added from below so that it is hidden.

Crochet Braiding

Picture 10-7; Crochet using water wave

This is a braided weave; it is one of the most effective protective styles in braiding once done properly and can last up to 3 months. It is applied to nearly every type of single braiding that exists and can give more natural looks as well.

The first step to crochet braiding is installing cornrows. A cornrow is a continuation of a plait along a given path, with that being said you start a cornrow the same way you will start a plait but you just keep your knuckles pressed down to the clients hair throughout the plait. After each rotation you grab up hair directly under to ensure that it does not lift and continue throughout. Always use small portions of hair and plait in the center of the plait see picture 10-8a. Cornrows should not be done too small as it will cause the style to take extremely long. After installing Cornrows stitch loose ends up as shown in picture 10-8b.

Picture 10-8a    Picture 10-8b

The second step is to use the interlocking needle and pass hair through the cornrow. Next, you must bend the hair in half and place the loop at the top in the hook. Then close the loop, and pass the needle back under the cornrow. Then pass only one of the braid ends through the loop twice to lock.

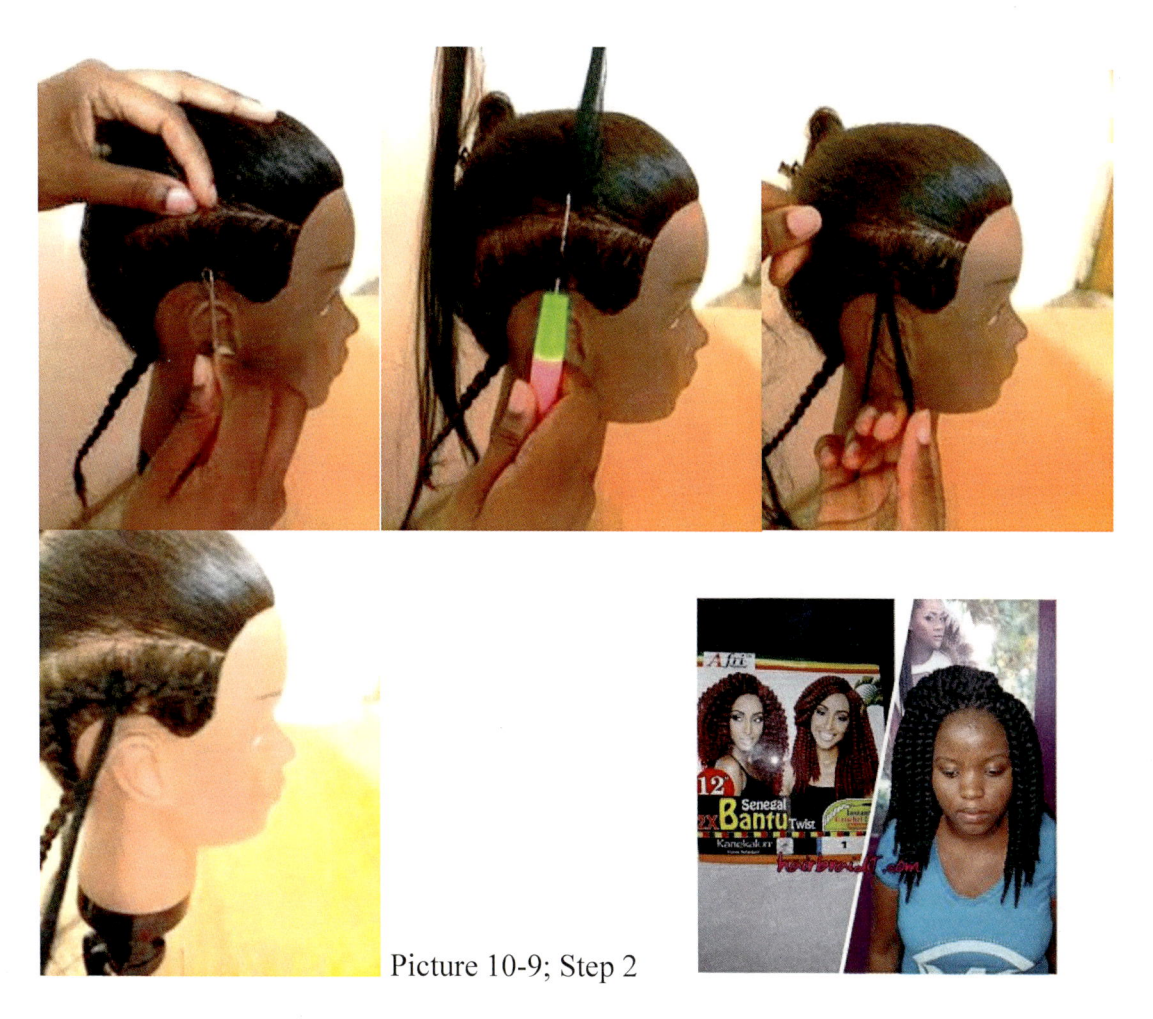

Picture 10-9; Step 2

Picture 10-10; Pre-Twisted Crochet.

Goddess Braids

Picture 10-11; Goddess cornrows

This is a quick easy and elegant style to extend your hair before getting a full re-do. It is braiding from the inside, basically the opposite of what you have just learnt. Some people simple call is inside cornrows

Step 1: part hair in the desired style

Picture 10-12; Step 1

Step 2: part a small section across the base of the style and a guide down the center of the desired plait.

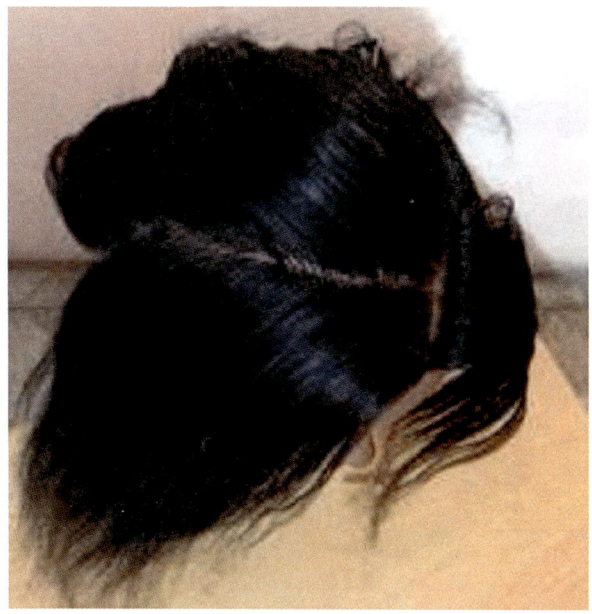

Picture 10-13; Step 2

Step 3: Make a full inside rotation with the small section at the top and take the piece of hair from the end and carry to the middle of the other two pieces, then take the piece on the other far end and carry it to the middle of the other two pieces.

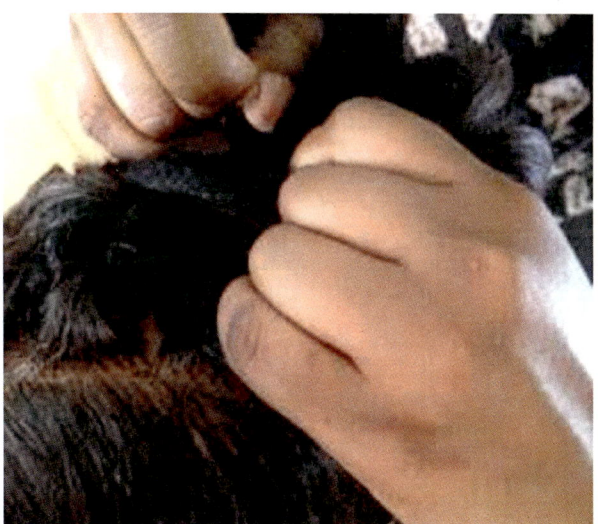

Picture 10-14; Step 3

Step 4: Follow the plait down the center of the given part ensuring that knuckles are pressed tightly to the client's hair, and continue to pick up pieces along the way.

11. Braiding Don'ts

As a professional hair stylist understanding the technique is not the only important factor. It is important for you to understand hair, as well as the client's needs and wants. This will ensure that you will effectively give the client the protective style they desire. Below are some pointers you should keep in mind when you have to advise a client or maintain a successful appointment.

- Never install braids when a client's hair is wet. Always ensure it is fully dried, or else the hair can break when unloosing the braid.
- One of the pieces may thin out at the end of the plait or twist because it was too short. Simply keep holding the braids tightly, take piece from one of the thicker pieces and transfer to the other one.
- When doing afro-kinky or Jamaican braids the twists might not look full. Simply unloose and twist in the other direction.
- If you portion the braid too thick, the client may not be able to control their braids. But if you do it too thin, it looks spacy. Some people's hair is very thin, so there is not much you can do however, your goal is to get the braids to look thick without it damaging her hair.
- The cornrows below crochet braids may show because they were done too big and there is not enough braid coverage.
- If you are not able to tease the hair properly the ends may unloose.
- With a thin hairline, you do not want to braid the hair too tightly, thus Try not to grip hair as tightly.
- Always make sure that the two ends of the plait meet when you start. This will ensure that the final plait is even.

12. Finishing the style

Picture 12.1; Curled ends

Kankelon braids are manipulated by boiling water. This helps to create new shapes like crimped, curled and straight ends.

When dipping the ends, always use boiling water and a container/mug with a handle that can hold all the water from the kettle.

Make sure all the hair is tied together; always try to use a rubber band. When dipping the braids do not leave the hair in the water for a long period of time, dip quickly and then remove from water.

> I. To create curled ends apply flexi rods or Jerri curl rods to the ends. Place hair over the mug and throw boiling water so that it covers the hair completely. Then towel dry and blow dry until hair is no longer dripping and remove rods in the direction of the curl.

II. To create straight ends, place hair over the mug and throw boiling water so that it covers the hair completely. Then use a towel to pull the braids down, and release once or twice quickly. If you are not satisfied, repeat the procedure till the ends are silky straight.

III. To get crimped ends, section the hair into small sections and create plaits with the braid. Place hair over the mug and throw boiling water so that it covers the hair completely. Towel dry and blow dry and then unloose plaits.

After one of the three above options is completed clip off any stringy ends and apply mouse, hair spray or any other products for the desired style.

See youtube video; How to dip the ends of kankelon braids.

✓ **Part 4- Professionalism**

13. Salon set up

Stylists please invest in your salon. Along with all the general tools ensure that you have the proper equipment that will allow your service to be completed more efficiently.

Essential equipment includes:

Must haves:

Hydraulic chair-fully adjustable

Hairdressing station/table

Optional:

This list will allow you to offer complimentary services which may possibly increase your income and services.

Shampoo sink

Hair dryer

Waiting chair

14. Time management

Time management is crucial to your craft, braiding takes long periods of times this will help with your pricing, scheduling appointments and managing your home duties.

Here are some ideas you should implement;

- ➢ Booking appointments
- ➢ Late fees

- Cancelation fees
- Down payments
- Online forms
- Appointment books

It is important that you learn to make time to rest, relax and exercise, as in the hair industry nearly every part of the body is at risk. Regular pains and discomforts are experienced while performing daily tasks, so it is important that you take care of your health.

Time yourself each time you style a client, and try to keep 30minutes to an hour rest period in between braid appointments.

15. The client

Always greet the client on the first meeting, ask them how they are and find out the service that they need. See client consultation card below.

	Braid Consultation
	Name Number Email Date and time of appointment Client's hair texture Length of the client's hair Any hair and scalp conditions Braid style you desire Size of the braid Colour braid you desire Length of the braid

16. Running a business

<u>Perfecting</u>

- ✓ Time yourself at all times. Determine your fastest time and try to stick to it. For each major section of hair determine how long you should or will take on it and try to stick to that time.
- ✓ Treat each client's hair differently and as a new learning experience, always try to find a better way to do the same thing.
- ✓ Determine if a person's hair is too thin or too thick to use regular parting techniques and the amount of hair used. A little more or less hair may be required as well as smaller or bigger parts. Take great precaution when parting a person's hairline especially when it is thin, yes we want the hair to look neat but we also want to promote healthy hair.
- ✓ Be careful with colour: some love it, some like it and some hate it, do not force anyone to put in a colour and determine if you are putting in too much or too little colour to suit a client's personality.

<u>Pricing</u>

- ✓ Most plait styles using the three strand method tend to last much longer, these styles take very long to install and you usually find that they have higher costs of labour.
- ✓ Twists styles and cornrow styles usually have lower labour costs because they may not stay neat as long as the plait method. They often require a touch up or we get more frequent visits from the clients.

Money management

You are your own boss; you are required to save for yourself, pay yourself and re-invest in yourself. Open bank accounts, credit union accounts and insurance accounts for security. Always be open to learning something new and keep educating yourself about hair and other important, equipment, tools and products that exist.

Review Questions

1. Products used

Match a hairstyle from column one with a product from column two.

Column one	Column two
Patra	Hair Mousse
Nubian locks	Hair jam
Freetress curls	Weave Glue/ lighter

Products used.

Place a ✓ by the products that can be used to do twists and an X by the products that cannot be used.

Let's Jam   _____

Jet's Gel   _____

Via Natural Style Jam _____

Shine   _____

Hair Grease   _____

Beeswax   _____

Edge Control   _____

2. Name two braiding don'ts.

3. Give a worded description for the colour 33.

4. Give an outline of the two major steps to do crochet braiding?

5. Explain how to prepare braids for patra & box braid hairstyle.

6. List two things that can go wrong when doing twists?

7. What do you have to do from beginning to end for each twist to make sure it does not unravel?

8. What type of hair is commonly bought by clients, but cannot be used to do Senegalese twists from the roots?

9. What are the two lengths offered for jumbo twists and why?

10. How many packs of hair do you need to do the following lengths in Senegalese twists?

11. Short_____

12. Medium_____

13. Long_____

14. List 5 tools you need to complete the client's hair

15. Name three brands/types of braids which can give the client a natural look. (Do not name styles please name the braiding hair.)

Creating your business exercise!

1. Create a business name. This should reflect the services and ambience clients will receive at your shop. Try to make it short and catchy.

_____

2. Create a slogan for your business this will help to give clients a gentle reminder of what they should expect.

_____

Example; business name : Hair? Braid it!

Slogan; The braiding headquarters.

3. Create a mission statement. This statement will give a clear understanding of the growth you hope to achieve in the next 5-10 years.

Example. To create the first training facility for braiding that encourages individuals to become young entrepreneurs.

_____
_____
_____

4. List objectives and goals to attain your mission statement. This should clearly identify the steps you are willing to take to develop your business over the next couple years.

_____
_____
_____
_____